## *Part 1:* Learning Letters

Trace the letters and practice writing them in the remaining space.
Use the blank practice page to write on your own.

A is for Alligator

a a a a a a a a

a

a a a a a a a a a a a a

a

B is for bear

B B B B B B B B

B

b b b b b b b b b b b

b

C is for cat

D is for dog

D D D D D D D D

D

d d d d d d d d d d d d

d

E is for elephant

E

E

e

e

F is for frog

G is for giraffe

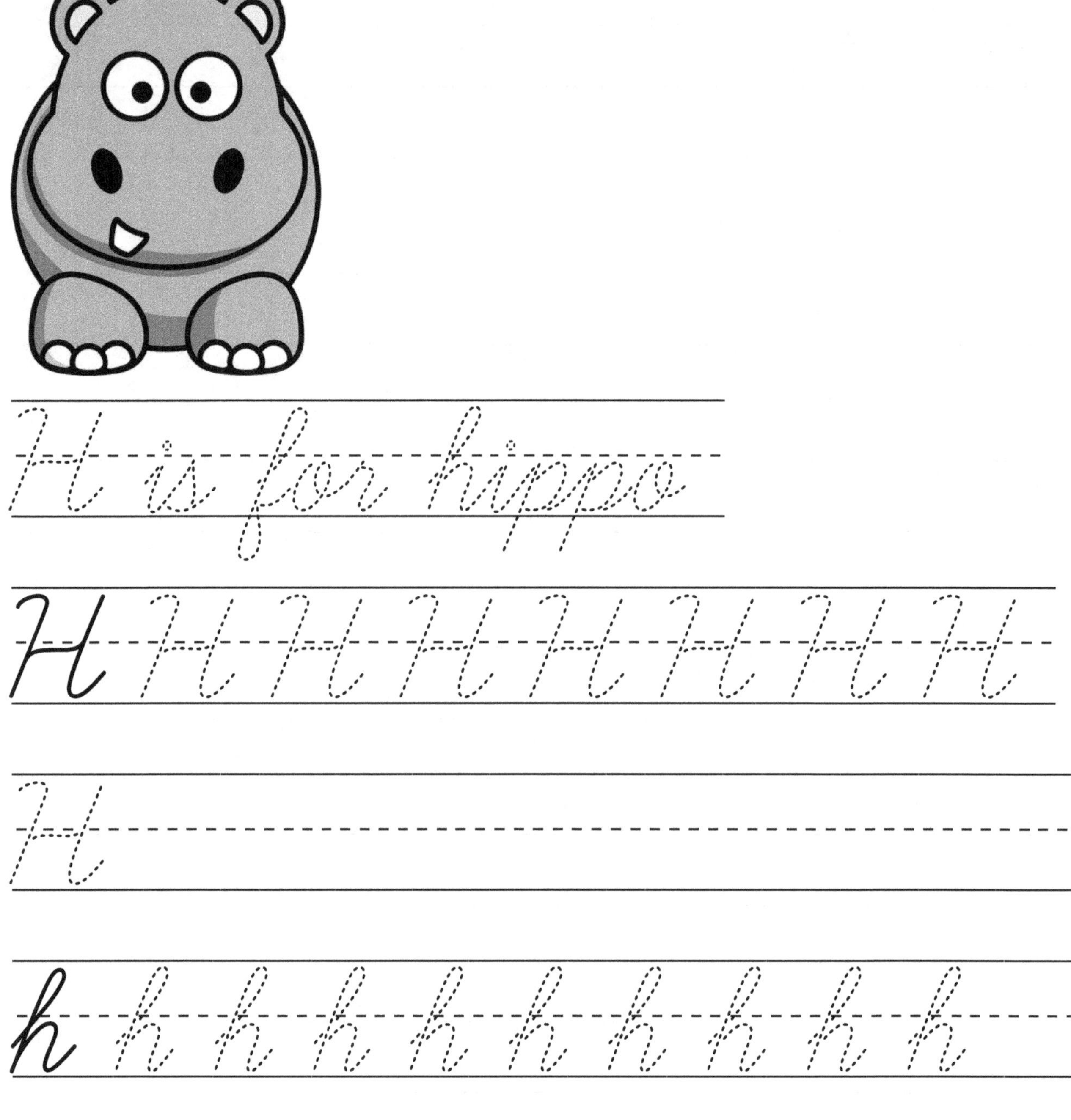

H is for hippo

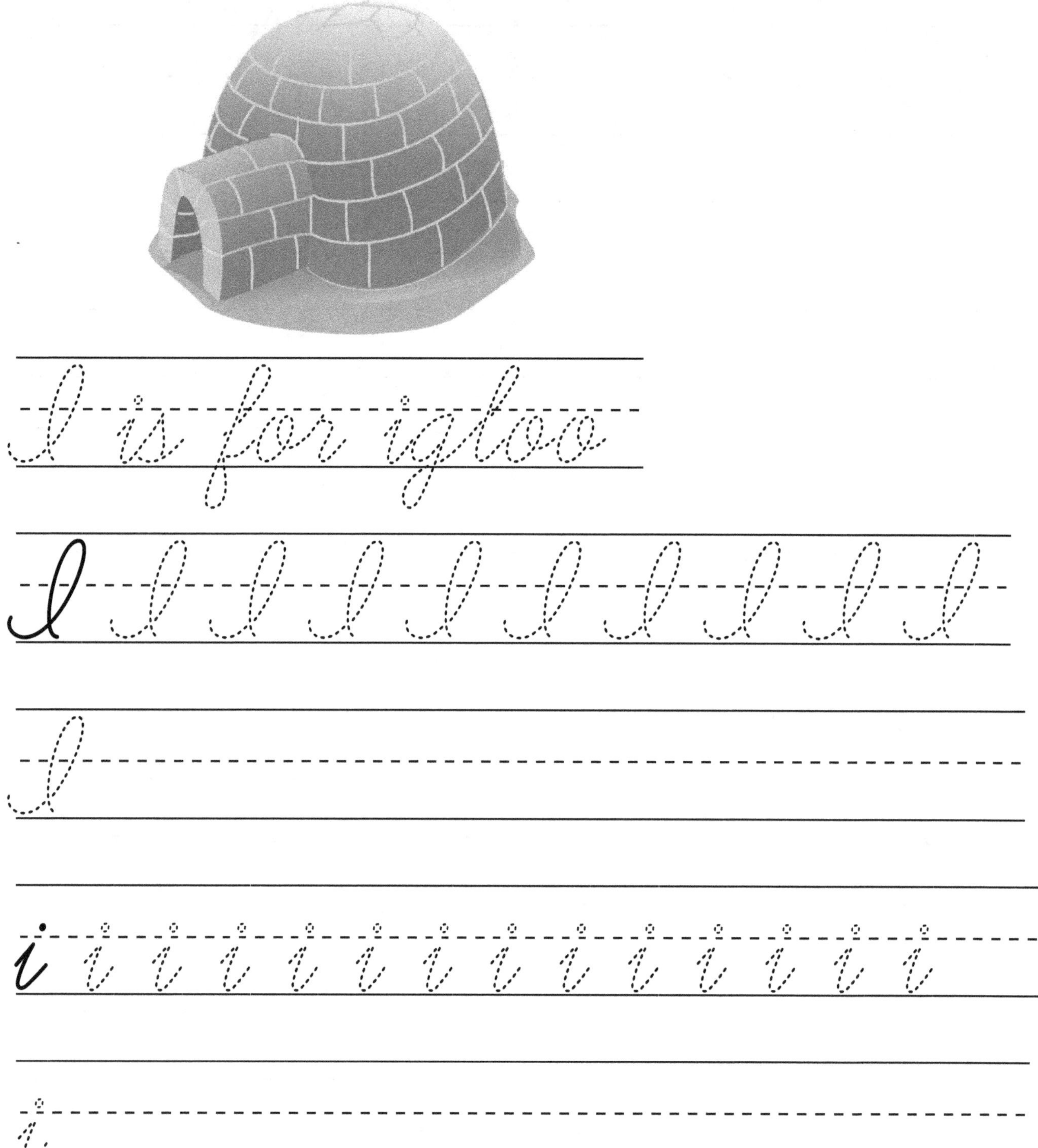

i is for igloo

*J is for jaguar*

$\mathcal{J}$ $\mathcal{J}$ $\mathcal{J}$ $\mathcal{J}$ $\mathcal{J}$ $\mathcal{J}$ $\mathcal{J}$ $\mathcal{J}$ $\mathcal{J}$

$j$ $j$ $j$ $j$ $j$ $j$ $j$ $j$ $j$ $j$ $j$ $j$ $j$

# K is for kangaroo

K K K K K K K K K

K

k k k k k k k k k k

k

L is for lion

M is for mouse

N is for net

N n n n n n n n

n

n n n n n n n n n

n

O is for owl

O O O O O O O

O

O O O O O O O O O O O

O

P is for panda

P P P P P P P P

P

p p p p p p p p p

p

# Q

2 is for question

R is for rabbit

R R R R R R R R R

R

r r r r r r r r r r r r

r

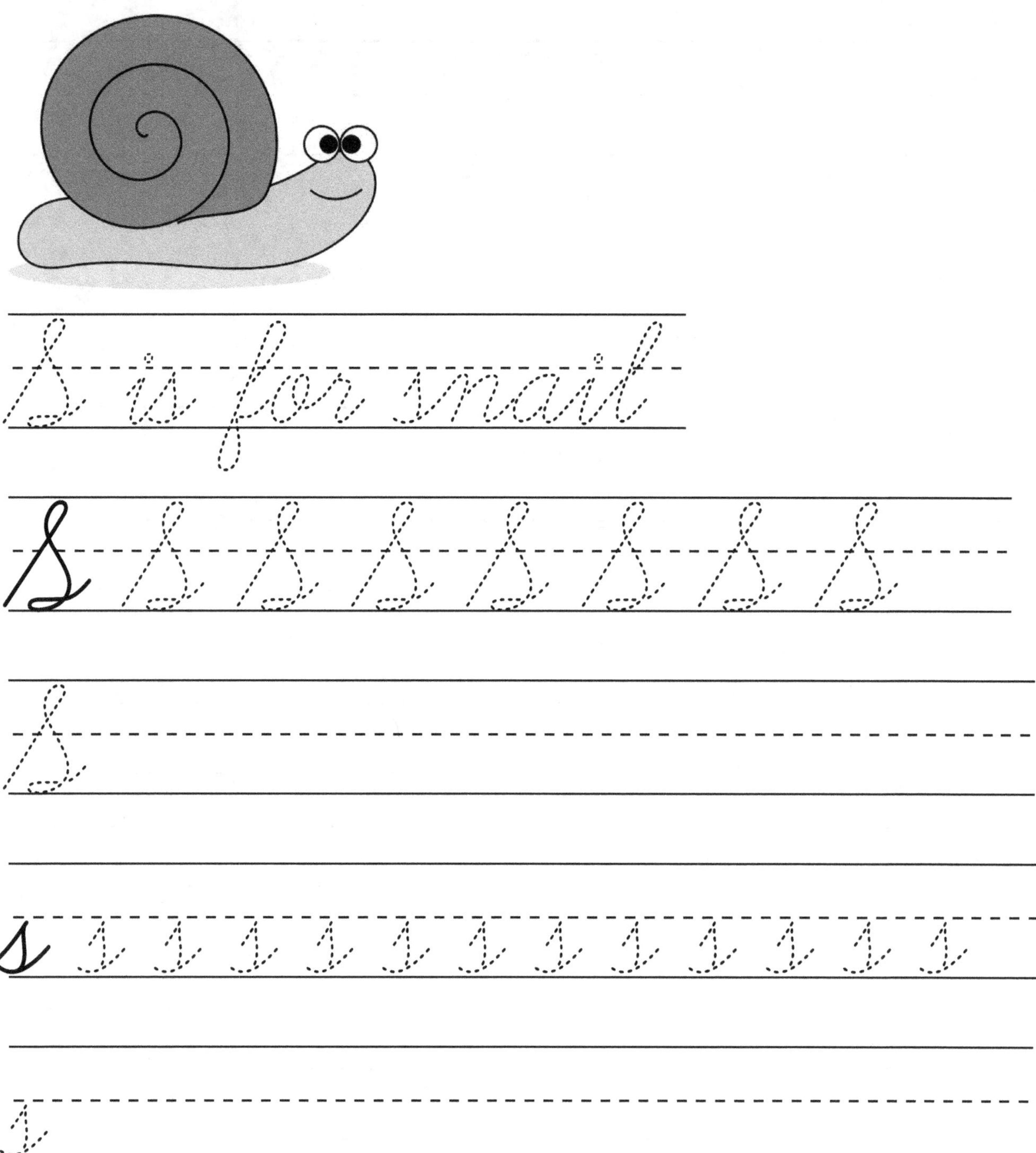

S is for snail

T is for tiger

T T T T T T T T

T

t t t t t t t t t t t t t

t

U is for unicorn

U U U U U U U

U

u u u u u u u u u u u

u

V is for vegtables

V V V V V V V V V

V

u u u u u u u u u

u

W is for whale

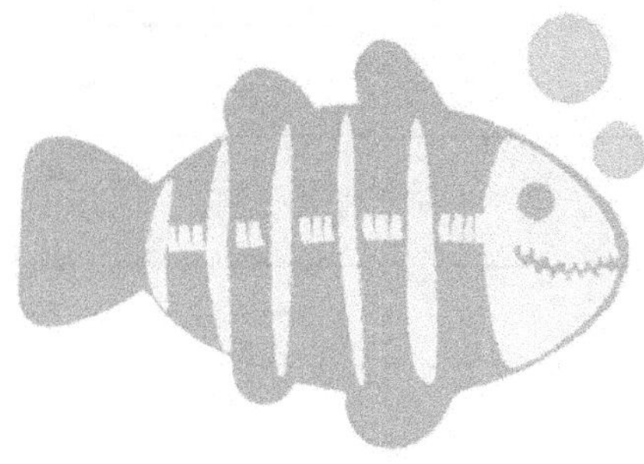

X is for x-ray

X X X X X X X X

X

x x x x x x x x x x x

x

Y is for yak

Y Y Y Y Y Y Y Y Y

Y

y y y y y y y y y

y

Z is for zebra

Z Z Z Z Z Z Z Z Z Z

Z

Z Z Z Z Z Z Z Z Z Z

Z

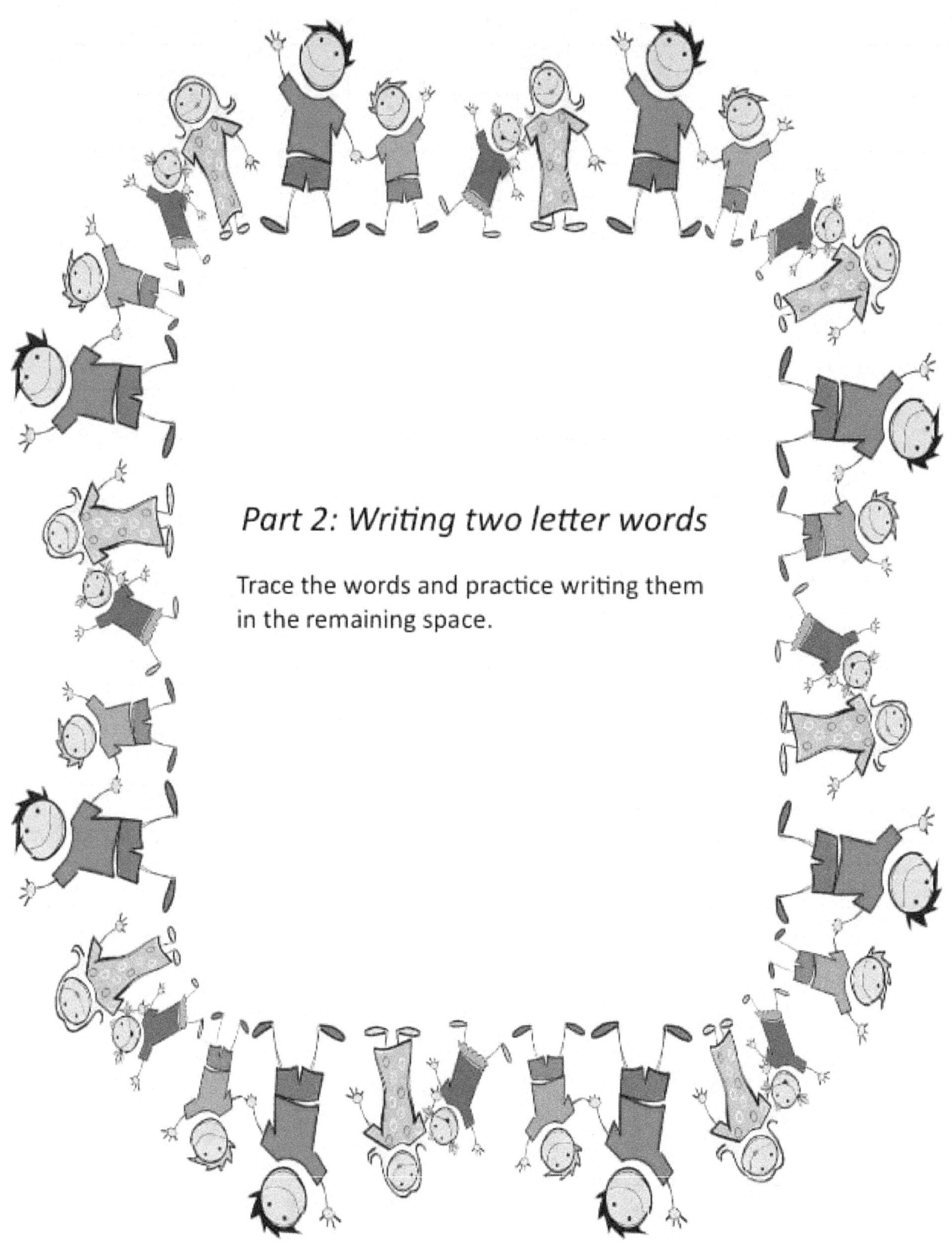

## Part 2: Writing two letter words

Trace the words and practice writing them in the remaining space.

go go go go go go go

go

he he he he he he he

he

ox ox ox ox ox ox ox

ox

do *do do do do do do*

*do*

it *it it it it it it it it*

*it*

no *no no no no no*

*no*

my my my my

my

be be be be be be be

be

so so so so so so so

so

at *at at at at at at*

*at*

am *am am am am am*

*am*

in *in in in in in in*

*in*

*hi* *hi* *hi* *hi* *hi* *hi* *hi*

*hi*

*ax* *ax* *ax* *ax* *ax* *ax*

*ax*

*or* *or* *or* *or* *or* *or* *or*

*or*

## Part 3: Writing three letter words

Trace the words and practice writing them in the remaining space.

cat *cat cat cat cat*

*cat*

mat *mat mat mat*

*mat*

sat *sat sat sat sat*

*sat*

bed *bed bed bed bed*

bed

led *led led led led*

led

fed *fed fed fed fed*

fed

fit fit fit fit fit fit fit

fit

wit wit wit wit wit

wit

hit hit hit hit hit hit

hit

pot *pot pot pot pot*

*pot*

got *got got got got*

*got*

hot *hot hot hot hot*

*hot*

fun fun fun fun fun

fun

run run run run

run

sun sun sun sun

sun

## Part 4: Writing four letter words

Trace the words and practice writing them in the remaining space.

boot *boot boot boot*

boot

pool *pool pool pool*

pool

foot *foot foot foot*

foot

heat *heat heat heat*

heat

feet *feet feet feet feet*

feet

live *live live live*

live

want *want want*

*want*

just *just just just just*

*just*

huge *huge huge huge*

*huge*

left *left left left left*

*left*

very *very very*

*very*

know *know know*

*know*

hook *hook hook hook*

*hook*

book *book book book*

*book*

wool *wool wool*

*wool*

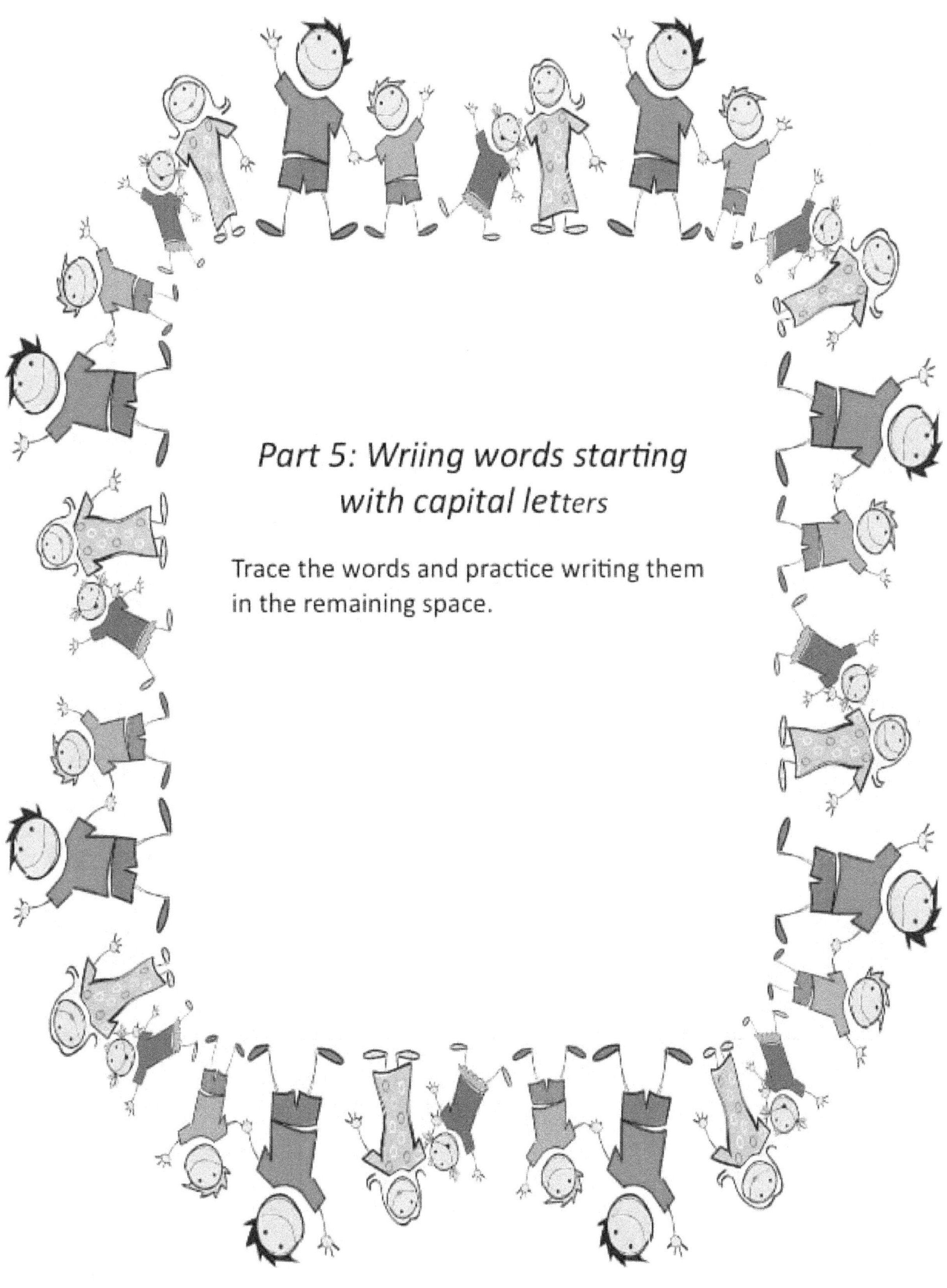

Part 5: Wriing words starting with capital letters

Trace the words and practice writing them in the remaining space.

Go Go Go Go Go

Go

Be Be Be Be Be Be

Be

It It It It It It

It

Or Or Or Or Or Or

Or

As As As As As As

As

In In In In In

In

Cat Cat Cat Cat Cat

Cat

Dog Dog Dog Dog

Dog

Fog Fog Fog Fog

Fog

Tub Tub Tub Tub

Tub

Not Not Not Not

Not

Can Can Can Can

Can

Grow Grow Grow

Grow

This This This This

This

Only Only Only

Only

Part 6: Writing numbers and
number words

Trace the words and writing them in the
remaining space

4 4 4 4 4 4 4 4 4 4

4

5 5 5 5 5 5 5 5 5 5

5

6 6 6 6 6 6 6 6 6 6

6

One One One One

One

Two Two Two Two

Two

Three Three Three

Three

Four Four Four

Four

Five Five Five

Five

Six Six Six Six

Six

Seven Seven Seven

Seven

Eight Eight Eight

Eight

Nine Nine Nine

Nine